LEVEL 2

Rainforests

Andrea Silen

NATIONAL GEOGRAPHIC

Washington, D.C.

For Mom and Dad, who taught me to explore —A.S.

Published by National Geographic Partners, LLC, Washington, D.C. 20036.

Designed by Yay! Design

Publisher's Note
The cover features a jaguar, the title page shows a toucan, and the Table of Contents page highlights a young tapir.

Library of Congress Cataloging-in-Publication Data

Names: Silen, Andrea, author.
Title: Rainforests / Andrea Silen.
Description: Washington, D.C. : National Geographic Kids, 2020. | Series: National geographic reader Level 2 | Audience: Ages 5-8 | Audience: Grades 2-3 | Summary: "Find out what a rainforest is and what kinds of plants and animals call the rainforests home"-- Provided by publisher.
Identifiers: LCCN 2019055278 (print) | LCCN 2019055279 (ebook) | ISBN 9781426338380 (paperback) | ISBN 9781426338397 (library binding) | ISBN 9781426338403 (ebook) | ISBN 9781426338410 (ebook other)
Subjects: LCSH: Rain forest ecology--Juvenile literature.
Classification: LCC QH541.5.R27 S55 2020 (print) | LCC QH541.5.R27 (ebook) | DDC 577.34--dc23
LC record available at https://lccn.loc.gov/2019055278
LC ebook record available at https://lccn.loc.gov/2019055279

The author and publisher gratefully acknowledge the expert content review of this book by Christopher Kuhar, Ph.D., executive director, Cleveland Metroparks Zoo, and the literacy review of this book by Mariam Jean Dreher, professor of reading education, University of Maryland, College Park.

Photo Credits
AL = Alamy Stock Photo; AS = Adobe Stock; NG = National Geographic Image Collection; SC = Science Source; SS = Shutterstock
Cover, Steve Winter/NG; top border (throughout), Natalia/AS; vocabulary art (throughout), Doloves/AS; 1, aabeele/SS; 3, Eric Isselée/SS; 4-5, Matthew Williams-Ellis/robertharding/AS; 6, NG Maps; 7, sara_winter/AS; 8, mbruxelle/AS; 9, Carlyn Iverson/SC; 10, jdross75/AS; 11, Dirk Ercken/SS; 12, Gerry Ellis/Digital Vision; 13, Patrick Landmann/SC; 14, Fedor Selivanov/SS; 15, Michael Nichols/NG; 16, Wayne Lawler/SC; 17 (UP), Dawna Moore/AL; 17 (LO), Anna ART/AS; 18, dvulikaia/AS; 19, Wilm Ihlenfeld/SS; 20 (UP), prasitphoto/AS; 20 (LO), dennisvdwater/AS; 21, Roger de la Harpe/DanitaDelimont/AL; 22 (UP), Chansom Pantip/SS; 22 (CTR), Leagam/SS; 22 (LO), Martin Edstrom/NG; 23 (UP), Jesus Ocana/AS; 23 (CTR), Andrea Izzotti/SS; 23 (LO), Sarin Kunthong/SS; 25, My Good Images/SS; 26-27, Doug Gimesy/NG; 27, Michael Nichols/NG; 28, PhilipYb Studio/SS; 29, Florian Kopp/AL; 30 (UP), Mint Images/Paul Edmondson/SC; 30 (CTR), Carlyn Iverson/SC; 30 (LO leopard), Sarah Cheriton-Jones/SS; 30 (LO chameleon), Fedor Selivanov/SS; 30 (LO gorilla), Michael Nichols/NG; 30 (LO beetle), Simon Shim/SS; 31 (UP LE frog), Jak Wonderly/SS; 31 (UP LE butterfly), Jesus Ocana/AS; 31 (UP LE elephant), Michael Nichols/NG; 31 (UP LE tree), Oscity/SS; 31 (UP RT), M Rutherford/SS; 31 (LO LE), Michael Nichols/NG; 31-27 (LO RT), Doug Gimesy/NG; 32 (UP LE), Gerry Ellis/Digital Vision; 32 (UP RT), Photographer/AL; 32 (CTR), Gudkov Andrey/SS; 32 (LO LE), Stas Moroz/SS; 32 (LO RT), Paul Zahl/NG

National Geographic supports K–12 educators with ELA Common Core Resources. Visit natgeoed.org/commoncore for more information.

Printed in the United States of America
20/WOR/1

Table of Contents

Rainforests Rule!

Rain drips down the trees. Monkeys howl. Birds with big green beaks fly by. Welcome to the rainforest!

Rainforests have towering trees, lots of plants, and colorful animals. People live there, too. Rainforests are wet places. In some rainforests, it rains almost every day of the year!

the Amazon rainforest in South America

Rainforests Around the World

Rainforests do not cover much of Earth's land. But they are found all over the world, except in Antarctica.

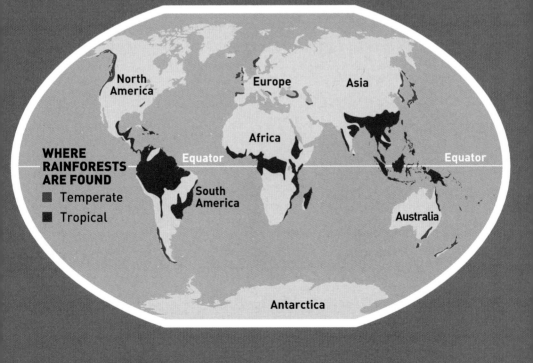

North America

Europe

Asia

Africa

WHERE RAINFORESTS ARE FOUND
- Temperate
- Tropical

Equator

South America

Equator

Australia

Antarctica

Most rainforests grow in warm, wet areas near the Equator (ih-KWAY-tur). These are tropical rainforests. Rainforests in cooler areas are called temperate (TEM-pur-it) rainforests.

Rainforest Talk

TROPICAL: Having hot, wet weather throughout the year

TEMPERATE: Not very cold or very hot throughout the year

a temperate rainforest in Victoria, Australia

Lots of Layers

Tropical rainforests have four layers. Each layer gets a different amount of sunlight, wind, and rain. This makes each layer a good home for different plants and animals.

Lobster claw flowers are found in the understory layer.

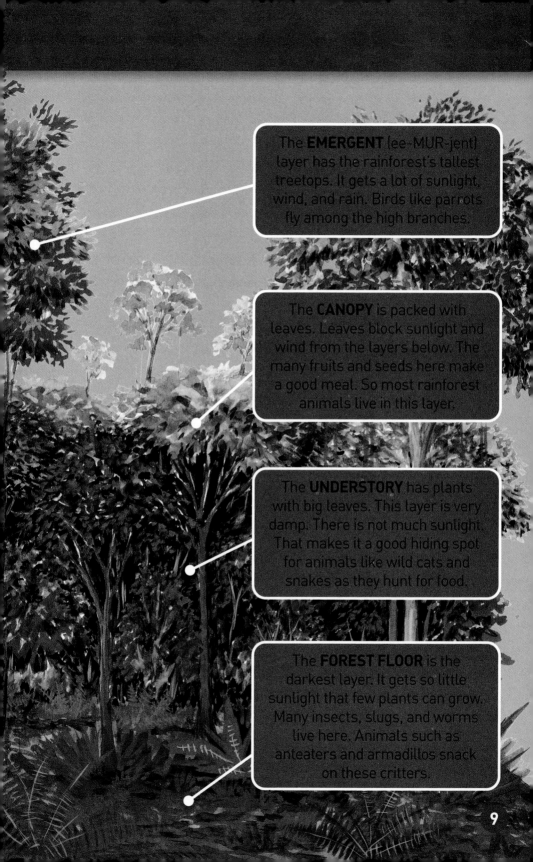

The **EMERGENT** (ee-MUR-jent) layer has the rainforest's tallest treetops. It gets a lot of sunlight, wind, and rain. Birds like parrots fly among the high branches.

The **CANOPY** is packed with leaves. Leaves block sunlight and wind from the layers below. The many fruits and seeds here make a good meal. So most rainforest animals live in this layer.

The **UNDERSTORY** has plants with big leaves. This layer is very damp. There is not much sunlight. That makes it a good hiding spot for animals like wild cats and snakes as they hunt for food.

The **FOREST FLOOR** is the darkest layer. It gets so little sunlight that few plants can grow. Many insects, slugs, and worms live here. Animals such as anteaters and armadillos snack on these critters.

Animals Everywhere

Most clouded leopards live in rainforests in parts of Asia.

Animals live in every layer of a tropical rainforest. Let's meet some cool rainforest critters!

Clouded leopards use their big paws and sharp claws to climb trees. From the branches, they can pounce onto prey on the ground below.

Poison dart frogs ooze poison from their skin. Their bright colors warn predators to stay away.

Rainforest Talk

PREY: An animal that is eaten by another animal

PREDATOR: An animal that hunts and eats other animals

Poison dart frogs are from Central and South American rainforests.

Keel-billed toucans live in Central and South America.

Keel-billed toucans are arboreal (are-BORE-ee-ul). They live in the forest canopy. They pluck fruit from the trees with their beaks. Then they toss the fruit in the air and catch it in their mouths.

Titan beetles can be found in parts of South America.

Titan (TIE-ten) beetles can grow bigger than your hand. Their jaws bite hard enough to break a pencil in half!

Rainforest Talk

ARBOREAL: Living in trees

Panther chameleons live in Madagascar, an island off the coast of Africa.

Panther chameleons (cuh–MEEL–yens) grip onto tree branches with their toes. Their sticky tongues shoot out to catch insects. These chameleons can also change color to scare or show off to other chameleons.

Gorillas play during the day. They also nap and munch on plants. At night, they sleep in nests made of branches and leaves.

Gorillas are from Africa.

15

Plenty of Plants

Tropical rainforests are not only filled with animals. They're also packed with plants. Vines wrap around trees. Flowers bloom on shrubs and tree trunks.

Big vines grow in some rainforests.

Rainforest plants are important. They make oxygen (OX-uh-jen), a gas that is part of the air. Living things need oxygen to breathe.

passionflower

The rafflesia (ruh-FLEE-jah) is the largest flower in the world. It smells like rotten meat!

Trees and plants soak up rainwater to live. In the rainforest, they can put water back into the air around them, too.

Tiny holes in the leaves let water escape. The water goes back into the air and forms clouds. The clouds keep the rainforest warm and damp, even when there is no rain.

Famous Forests

a giraffe weevil in the Amazon rainforest

The world's largest tropical rainforest is in South America. It's called the Amazon rainforest. More kinds of plants and animals live there than anywhere else on Earth.

The Congo rainforest in Africa is the second largest rainforest. It has big animals like forest elephants and chimps. Both rainforests are home to rare wildlife. This makes them important habitats.

an African forest elephant in the Congo rainforest

Rainforest Talk

HABITAT: The place where an animal or plant naturally lives

6 COOL FACTS About Rainforests

1 Rainforest vines called lianas (LEE-ah-nahs) can grow about as long as an American football field.

More than 3,000 kinds of fruit are found in rainforests.

2

dragon fruit

One big cave in Vietnam has its own rainforest.

Hang Son Doong cave in Vietnam

3

The glasswing butterfly from Central American rainforests has see-through wings.

4

5

One type of monkey in the rainforest grows a huge mustache.

emperor tamarin

More than half of the world's animals live in rainforests.

6

stork-billed kingfisher

23

Keep It Cool

Temperate rainforests are cooler than tropical ones. They also get less rain. Most rain falls in winter. In summer, most of these forests fill with fog from nearby oceans or seas. This keeps the forests damp.

Trees in these rainforests can be very tall. Redwood trees in North America can grow over 300 feet high—taller than the Statue of Liberty!

Huge redwood trees make an adult look small.

25

Tawaki penguins are one of the rarest types of penguins.

Temperate rainforests are also full of animals. Some are common, like mice, snakes, and owls. Others might surprise you.

Q Why did the rainforest take a class?

A It wanted to branch out.

Banana slugs can grow up to eight inches long!

Slugs that look like bananas live in rainforests in the United States. In New Zealand's rainforests, penguins called tawaki (TAH-wah-kee) make nests for their young.

Rainforest Rescue

Rainforest trees are often cut down for wood. They are also cleared away to make room for farms. Luckily, many people are working to protect these forests. People are planting new trees, too.

Many rainforest trees were cut down and burned so that crops could be planted.

Rainforests are amazing places. They are home to lots of plants and animals. So it is important to keep them safe.

In this part of the Amazon rainforest, all of the old trees were cut down. Now farmers care for newly planted trees.

QUIZ WHIZ

How much do you know about rainforests? After reading this book, probably a lot! Take this quiz and find out.

Answers are at the bottom of page 31.

How are temperate rainforests different from tropical ones?

A. They are warmer.
B. They are cooler.
C. They are wetter.
D. none of the above

1

2

Which layer of the rainforest is the darkest?

A. emergent layer
B. canopy layer
C. understory layer
D. forest floor layer

Which of these rainforest animals sleeps in nests made of branches and leaves?

A. clouded leopard
B. panther chameleon
C. titan beetle
D. gorilla

3

4

Which of these can you find in the Congo rainforest?

A. redwood trees
B. forest elephants
C. glasswing butterflies
D. poison dart frogs

How many types of fruit are found in rainforests?

A. more than 30
B. more than 300
C. more than 3,000
D. more than 30,000

5

6

Some of the slugs in U.S. rainforests look like _____.

A. bananas
B. carrots
C. cucumbers
D. apples

What type of penguins live in New Zealand's rainforests?

A. emperor penguins
B. chinstrap penguins
C. king penguins
D. tawaki penguins

7

ARBOREAL: Living in trees

HABITAT: The place where an animal or plant naturally lives

PREDATOR: An animal that hunts and eats other animals

PREY: An animal that is eaten by another animal

TEMPERATE: Not very cold or very hot throughout the year

TROPICAL: Having hot, wet weather throughout the year